A Note to Parents

DK READERS is a compelling program for beginning readers, designed in conjunction with leading literacy experts, including Dr. Linda Gambrell, Professor of Education at Clemson University. Dr. Gambrell has served as President of the National Reading Conference, College Reading Association, and has recently been elected to serve as President of the International Reading Association.

Beautiful illustrations and superb full-color photographs combine with engaging, easy-to-read stories to offer a fresh approach to each subject in the series. Each DK READER is guaranteed to capture a child's interest while developing his or her reading skills, general knowledge, and love of reading.

The five levels of DK READERS are aimed at different reading abilities, enabling you to choose the books that are exactly right for your child:

Pre-level 1: Learning to read
Level 1: Beginning to read
Level 2: Beginning to read alone
Level 3: Reading alone
Level 4: Proficient readers

The "normal" age at which a child begins to read can be anywhere from three to eight years old, so these levels are only a general guideline.

No matter which level you select, you can be sure that you are helping your child learn to read, then read to learn!

DK

LONDON, NEW YORK, MUNICH,
MELBOURNE, and DELHI

Series Editor Penny Smith
Art Editor Leah Germann
U.S. Editors Elizabeth Hester, John Searcy
DTP Designer Almudena Díaz
Production Angela Graef
Picture Research Myriam Megharbi
Dinosaur Consultant Dougal Dixon

Reading Consultant
Linda Gambrell, Ph.D.

First American Edition, 2006
10 11 12 13 10 9
Published in the United States by DK Publishing, Inc.
375 Hudson Street, New York, New York 10014

DK books are available at special discounts for bulk purchases for sale promotions,
premiums, fundraising, or educational use. For details, contact:
DK Publishing Special Markets
375 Hudson Street
New York, NY 10014
SpecialSales@dk.com

Library of Congress Cataloging-in-Publication Data
Meet the dinosaurs.-- 1st American ed.
p. cm. -- (DK readers. Pre-level 1, Learning to read)
ISBN-13 978-0-7566-1910-7 (pb)
ISBN-13 978-0-7566-1911-4 (hb)
1. Dinosaurs--Juvenile literature. I. Series: Dorling Kindersley readers. Pre-level 1,
Learning to read.
QE861.5.M437 2006
567.9--dc22
2005032704

Color reproduction by Colourscan, Singapore
Printed and bound in China by L Rex Printing Co., Ltd.

The publisher would like to thank the following for their kind permission
to reproduce their photographs:
a=above; c=center; b=below; l=left; r=right; t=top; b/g=background

Alamy Images: Robert Harding Picture Library Ltd 20-21 b/g, 31cr b/g. **Corbis:** Matt
Brown 26-27 b/g; Larry Lee Photography 18-19 b/g, 30cl b/g; W. Wayne Lockwood, MD
4-5c b/g, 8-9 b/g; Charles Mauzy 5tcl b/g, 24-25 b/g; Craig Tuttle 4br b/g, 14-15 b/g, 16-
17 b/g, 28-29 b/g, 31bcl b/g; Jim Zuckerman 6-7, 30cb b/g. **DK Images:** Jon Hughes 4-5c,
8-9. **Getty Images:** J.P. Nacivet 22-23 b/g, 31tr b/g; James Randklev 4c b/g, 10-11 b/g.

All other images © Dorling Kindersley
For more information see: www.dkimages.com

Discover more at

www.dk.com

DK READERS

Meet the Dinosaurs

DK Publishing, Inc.

Watch out!
Here come
the dinosaurs.

Here is the scary Tyrannosaurus [tuh-RAN-oh-SORE-us]. It has sharp teeth.

Tyrannosaurus

teeth

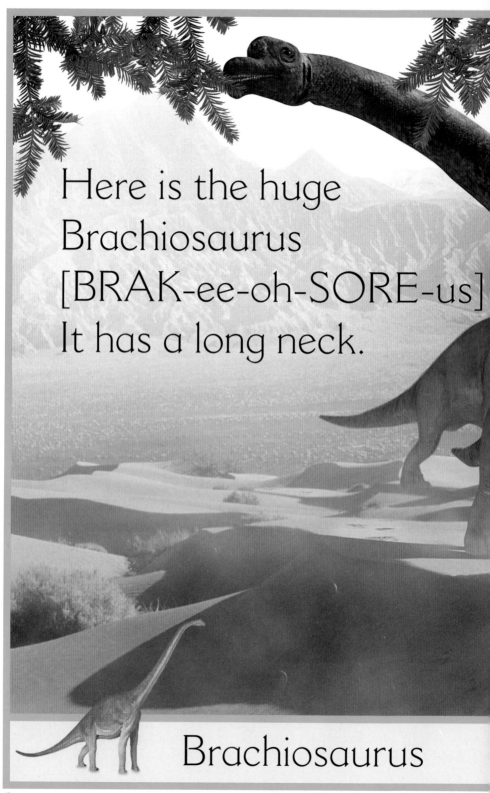

Here is the huge
Brachiosaurus
[BRAK-ee-oh-SORE-us]
It has a long neck.

Brachiosaurus

neck

Here is the tough
Triceratops
[try-SAIR-uh-tops].
It has three horns.

Triceratops

horn

Here is the fierce
Velociraptor
[vuh-LOSS-uh-rap-ter].
It has sharp claws.

Velociraptor

claw

crest

Corythosaurus

Here is the noisy Corythosaurus [ko-RITH-oh-SORE-us]. It has a bright crest.

Here is the small Compsognathus [KOMP-sug-NAY-thus]. It runs fast.

foot

Compsognathus

Here is the clever
Troodon
[TRO-oh-don].
It has large eyes.

Troodon

eye

Here is the spiky
Stegosaurus
[STEG-oh-SORE-us].
It has a very small brain.

head

Stegosaurus

Here is the
bird-like Gallimimus
[GAL-uh-MIME-us].
It has thin legs
and a beak.

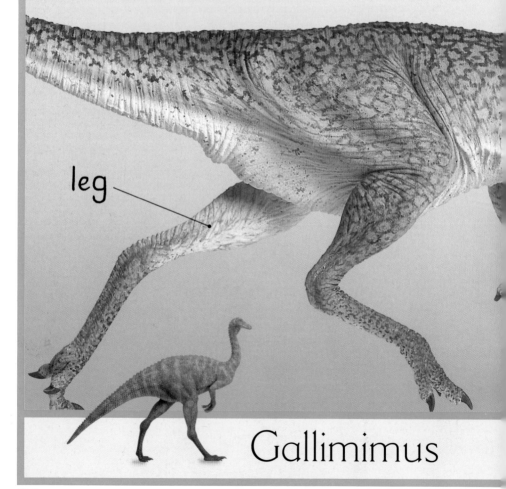

leg

Gallimimus

beak

spike

Iguanodon

Here is the strong iguanodon [ig-WAHN-oh-don].
It has a spike on each thumb.

Here is the plant-eater,
Stegoceras
[ste-GOSS-er-us].
It has a thick skull.

skull

Stegoceras

Here is the armored
Ankylosaurus
[ANG-kuh-low-SORE-us]
It has a tail club.

Ankylosaurus

club

Which dinosaur
do you like best?
The one who is…

clever?

scary?

bird-like?

spiky?

noisy?

Picture word list

Tyrannosaurus
page 6

Brachiosaurus
page 8

Triceratops
page 10

Velociraptor
page 12

Corythosaurus
page 14

Compsognathus
page 16

Troodon
page 18

Stegosaurus
page 20

Gallimimus
page 22

Iguanodon
page 24

Stegoceras
page 26

Ankylosaurus
page 28